THE GRAPES OF WRATH

by
John Steinbeck

Teacher Guide
Written by
Mary Lovejoy Dennis

Note

The Penguin Books paperback edition, © 1939 John Steinbeck, was used to prepare this guide. The page references may differ in other editions.

Please note: Please assess the appropriateness of this book for the age level and maturity of your students prior to reading and discussing it with your class.

ISBN 1-56137-299-4

To order, contact your local school supply store, or—

Novel Units, Inc.
P.O. Box 97
Bulverde, TX 78163-0097

Web site: www.educyberstor.com

Table of Contents

Background Information

Most of John Steinbeck's novels take place in California, where he was born in 1902 in the fertile Salinas Valley. His mother, a school teacher, began reading famous literature to him while he was a young child, and this fostered his later interest in writing.

Although Steinbeck attended Stanford University for five years, he never obtained a degree. His pursuit of a writing career in New York City proved unsuccessful, but he continued to write when he returned to California, and finally published his first novel, *Tortilla Flat,* in 1935.

Other novels include *In Dubious Battle, Of Mice and Men, Cannery Row, The Wayward Bus, East of Eden, The Short Reign of Pippin IV, Travels With Charley,* and of course, *The Grapes of Wrath.*

Steinbeck's novels get their realism from the author's practice of living and working with the people about whom he wrote. Before writing *The Grapes of Wrath,* Steinbeck literally became a migrant worker, roaming California in search of work, feeling the pangs of hunger, and living in the deplorable Hoovervilles.

The Grapes of Wrath was considered very controversial when it was first published. Religious leaders denounced it as obscene. Oklahomans resented the portrayal of their citizens and their state. Californians insisted they were not as cruel as the picture Steinbeck painted of them. Many people called Steinbeck a Communist. Still, the novel brought attention to the plight of the migrant workers. Those who supported Steinbeck and believed his novel told the truth were concerned enough to demand government action. As a novel of social protest, *The Grapes of Wrath* was a great success. As a movie, it is a classic. In today's catalog of literature, it ranks as a timeless work of art.

The novel is somewhat unusual in structure. The general story of the dust storms, the road west, shady business practices, and the migrant camps is told in chapters which alternate with the more specific story of one particular migrant family, the Joads. Students of the novel are thus given a factual history along with a fictionalized example of how the historic events affected one family. The Joads represent all migrants—and in fact all poor, uneducated people— in 1930s America.

Steinbeck was awarded the Nobel Prize for literature in 1962 for the total body of his works.

Summary of the Novel

Tom Joad is on his way home to his father's tenant farm after serving four years in prison. On the way, he meets Jim Casy, a former preacher who has also been away for some time and has decided that "all things are holy" so there is no more need to preach.

When they reach the Joad farm, they find it deserted but cultivated, even the dooryard. The only remaining neighbor, Muley Graves, explains that the land-owners are making all the sharecroppers leave the land. The dust storms have made the farms unprofitable, and now the land owners have bought tractors that can quickly do the work of many families. Tom's family is at Uncle John's, about eight miles away, preparing to leave for California, where they hope to find work picking fruit.

They have sold most of their belongings to opportunistic junk men, and Tom's younger brother, Al, has picked out a used truck. The family piles on the few household goods remaining. They butcher two pigs and salt down the meat to take along. There will be Ma and Pa Joad, Grampa and Granma, daughter Rose of Sharon and her husband, Connie, and the rest of the Joad children: Noah, Tom, Al, Ruthie, and Winfield. They hold a family conference and decide that Casy can go with them.

At the last minute, Grampa Joad—a cantankerous old fellow who has lived on the farm all his long life—refuses to go. Since they can't leave him behind, they drug him with little Winfield's earache medicine. The first night of their journey, Grampa dies of a stroke as if leaving the farm has killed him. Here the Joads meet the Wilsons, and the two families begin traveling together. Sairy Wilson is terribly sick, but immensely kind. After a few days travel, she is too sick to continue and the Joads leave her regretfully, insisting that her husband take some of their food and money. The Joads finally arrive in Needles, California, and camp by a river until they are told by a policeman to leave. Noah, who is "strange," decides he will live by the river, and he walks away down the bank.

Granma grows steadily sicker and weaker, talking to Grampa in her delirium and confusion. She dies one night as they are crossing the desert, but only Ma Joad knows that Granma has slipped away. She bravely waits until they arrive in California to tell the family, and although Granma must be buried in a pauper's grave, at least it's in a green and lovely valley.

Once in California, the Joads realize the rumors they've heard are true: there is not enough work for all the migrants who are there, camped in filthy "Hoovervilles" where disease and starvation are rampant. The local people hate the "Okies," and routinely burn down their camps and insult them. During an incident with the local sheriff, Tom gets involved in a fight and Casy takes the blame and goes to jail, reminding Tom that he has broken his parole by leaving Oklahoma and can't afford trouble. The sheriff lets the camp residents know he'll burn them out if they don't leave. In the meantime, Rose of Sharon's husband, Connie, has gotten cold feet about his impending fatherhood responsibilities and has disappeared.

The Joads are lucky enough to find space in a clean federal government camp, but there is no work in the area. At the government camp, there is a brief respite from the horrors of the "outside" world, and they learn more about the reality of their situation. The labor contractors know how hungry the people are, and they cut the wages accordingly, knowing the men will work for nearly nothing. There is talk of organizing, and this is what the local people fear most.

The Joads hear of work in a peach orchard to the north, and decide to leave the government camp. When they arrive at the orchard, there is a workers' strike in progress. Not realizing that they are strikebreakers, only that they are starving, they go through the guarded gates and go to work immediately. That night Tom goes out to talk to the strikers and is surprised to find that Jim Casy is their leader. Some local lawmen approach, and when Casy tells them they're "helping to starve kids," they kill him. Tom, enraged, kills one of the lawmen while another hits Tom with a pick handle. Tom gets away, but is now a wanted man, so the family must leave and Tom must stay hidden.
They are fortunate enough to find work picking cotton, and they live in a boxcar with another family.

Tom hides in a nearby cave, and one night when Ma takes him supper he tells her he's leaving. He's decided to carry on Casy's work.

About the time the cotton is picked out, a torrential rain begins, and Rose of Sharon goes into labor. The baby is stillborn. Uncle John, who is sent to bury it, sets it afloat in the water to serve as a symbol of what the rich have done to the poor. The water keeps rising, finally forcing the family to leave on foot as the car won't start. They find shelter in a barn, where a man is slowly starving to death as his son watches. As the novel ends, Rose of Sharon feeds the dying man from her breast.

About the Guide

The guide is divided into fifteen sections. Each section covers two chapters and includes questions for discussion and writing and a vocabulary list. Level I Questions relate to comprehension of events: who, what, when, why, where. Answers are provided. Level II Questions require more critical thinking and may ask students to state and support opinions, give examples, or find out more information from another source. Since these questions are open-ended for the most part, specific answers are not given. Also provided are five activity pages, a list of suggested research topics, and project ideas which extend the novel into other areas of the curriculum.

Pre-Reading Discussion

Some or all of the following activities may be used to introduce students to a study of *The Grapes of Wrath.*

- Engage the students in a discussion of farming. This could be done by having them relate first-hand experiences on an actual farm or experiences with a small garden or potted plants. What effect does drought have on crops?

- Have the students locate Oklahoma on a map of the United States. Discuss the topography of this area. Ask the students to think about what might happen if there was no rain for a long time, but lots of wind blowing across flat land. (Hint: In the '30s this area was called "The Great Dust Bowl.")

- Discuss the difference between a tenant and an owner. You may want to use a t-chart on the chalkboard. Students can relate to this by thinking about the differences between renting and owning a home. In the former situation, the landlord can make the tenants leave. What might cause this to happen? (non-payment of rent, improper behavior, building being torn down to build something else)

- Clarify the definition of tenant as it relates to *The Grapes of Wrath,* i.e. tenant farmer or sharecropper. What might cause the owner of a tenant farm to ask the tenant farmer to leave?

- Ask the students to consider the title. Have them define "wrath." Have them offer ideas as to what the book might be about.

- Have the students check the publication date of the novel (1939) and discuss economic conditions in the United States at that time.

Using Predictions in the Novel Unit Approach

We all make predictions as we read—little guesses about what will happen next, how the conflict will be resolved, which details given by the author will be important to the plot, which details will help to fill in our sense of a character. Students should be encouraged to predict, to make sensible guesses. As students work on predictions, these discussion questions can be used to guide them: What are some of the ways to predict? What is the process of a sophisticated reader's thinking and predicting? What clues does an author give us to help us in making our predictions? Why are some predictions more likely than others?

A predicting chart is for students to record their predictions. As each subsequent chapter is discussed, you can review and correct previous predictions. This procedure serves to focus on predictions and to review the stories.

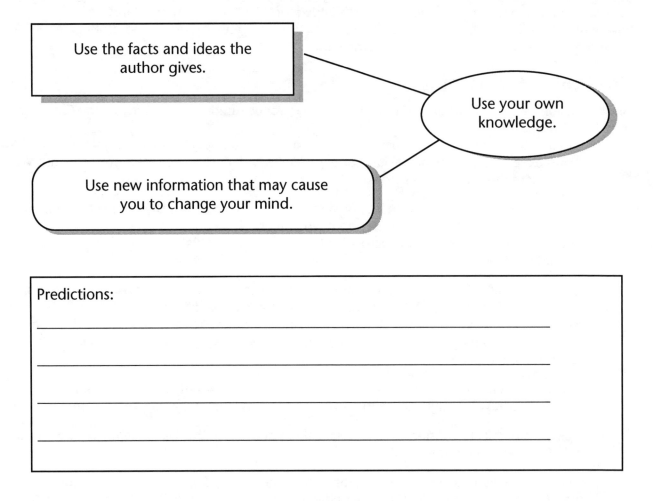

Use the facts and ideas the author gives.

Use your own knowledge.

Use new information that may cause you to change your mind.

Predictions:

_____

_____

_____

_____

Prediction Chart

What characters have we met so far?	What is the conflict in the story?	What are your predictions?	Why did you make those predictions?

Discussion Questions, Vocabulary, Writing Assignments and Activities

Chapters 1 and 2

Level I

1. When was the last rain? *(early May)*

2. Describe what happened to the corn. *(It faded and dried up.)*

3. What began to settle on everything? *(dust)*

4. Find the paragraph describing Tom Joad. Make a list of words that describe him. *(p. 9)*

5. What did the sign on the truck say? *("No Riders")*

6. Where has Tom been? *(McAlester Prison)* For how long? *(4 years)* Why? *(for homicide)*

7. What did the driver indirectly warn Tom about? *(the farmers being forced off their land)*

Level II

1. What would happen if the men "broke"? How would their faces have looked?

2. To what can you compare the dust storms?

3. The men didn't have much to do. Did they enjoy just sitting around?

4. Why did the driver give Tom a ride even though it was against company rules? Would you have done it? Do you think the driver regretted his decision?

5. What does "The driver's eyes slipped over Joad's face to memorize it" mean?

6. What do you think Tom will find at his father's farm?

Vocabulary

rivulet (3)	listless (8)	cowl (10)	dissipated (3)
protruded (9)	insinuation (12)	emulsion (5)	chambray (9)
judiciously (12)	bemused (6)	hobnailed (9)	subtle (12)
homicide (18)			

Writing Assignment

Write a paragraph describing how the area around your home changes because of weather. How does it look after a big snowstorm? How does it look after several days of rain? How does it look after not raining for a month?

Chapters 3 and 4

Level I

1. Who is the "character" in this chapter? *(a land turtle)*

2. What does the 40-year-old woman driver do? *(swerves to miss the turtle)*

3. What does the pickup driver do? *(swerves to hit the turtle)*

4. What does Tom pick up to bring to the kids? *(the turtle)*

5. Who does Tom see under the tree? *(Casy, the former preacher)*

6. List words describing Casy's appearance. *(pp. 24-25)*

7. What did Casy do while he was preaching that bothered him? *(had sexual relations with girls he had just "saved")*

8. How did Tom kill a man? *(The man knifed him at a dance; Tom hit him with a shovel.)*

9. What was good about prison? *(clean clothes, regular meals)* What was bad? *(no women)*

10. How did Pa Joad "steal" their house? *(When the family living in it moved, Pa and Tom's brother, Noah, cut it in half and dragged one half to their farm.)*

Level II

1. What do you think the turtle stands for?

2. What does the woman driver stand for?

3. What does the pickup driver stand for?

4. Why is it important that the turtle "planted" some seeds accidentally?

5. In what ways is the turtle admirable?

6. Discuss what Casy meant by "Got a lot of sinful idears but they seem kinda sensible."

7. Casy says words are just words; none of them are bad. Write a paragraph explaining why you do or do not agree.

8. Find out what Emerson's idea of the "oversoul" was and how Casy's ideas are similiar (p. 31).

9. What are Casy's ideas about sin and virtue? (p. 30) Do you agree?

10. Find the simile in the second paragraph on page 35. Think of a different way to complete the sentence. ("...plunged into the yellow sunlight like two swimmers hastening to get to shore.")

11. What kind of person do you think Uncle John is, judging from the story about the pig?

Vocabulary

fetlocks (19)	zenith (24)	hypocrite (28)
dispersed (19)	swale (24)	shoat (37)
anlage (19)	declivity (24)	parapet (20)
piqued (28)		

Writing Assignment

Some of Tom's former prison mates preferred prison life to home. Why? How do you think it would feel to be in jail? What would be the worst part?

Chapters 5 and 6

Level I

1. The owner men behaved in different ways. What were they? *(kind, angry, cold, proud)*

2. Why was the soil so poor? *(Cotton crops had ruined it.)*

3. What "point" did the owner men finally come to? *(The tenant system wouldn't work anymore.)*

4. Where did the owner men suggest the farmers go? *(California)*

5. What is Tom afraid has happened to his family? *(that they're all dead)*

6. How did Pa feel about writing? *(It gave him the shivers.)* Are the Joads educated people? *(no)*

7. Did the neighbors steal from Albert Rance? *(No. They thought he had left his farm permanently.)*

8. What information does Muley Graves give Tom and Casy? *(The family is at Uncle John's.)*

9. To what does Muley compare himself? *(a graveyard ghost)* What do you notice about his last name? *(Graves—grave yard—grave circumstances)*

10. Why is Tom not supposed to leave the state? *(He's on parole.)*

11. What did Casy do to make money in the past? *(He had a revival tent.)*

Level II

1. What is meant by "sunbeaten dooryard"? "corn-headed children"? What images do you get from these phrases?

2. In what way did the tenant farmers "own" the land?

3. How does Steinbeck compare the arrival of the tractors to an invasion by monsters? (p. 45)

4. What does Joe Davis' boy plan do as an "accident"? Why?

5. What is the connection between Chapters 5 and 6?

6. How was the cat a clue to Tom about the neighbors?

7. What can you tell about Grampa from Tom's comments? Give examples.

8. How does Muley explain his insistence on staying on the land? Have you ever felt similarly determined about something even though you knew it might be a bad decision?

9. What does Muley's monologue make Casy realize?

10. Do you think Tom's imprisonment accomplished anything? Explain your answer.

11. What is the difference between being a hunter and being the hunted? Who has the psychological advantage?

Vocabulary

scrabbled (41)	petulant (58)	truculently (60)
ravenously (68)	convulsed (68)	

Writing Assignment

Tom says he knew things wouldn't be the same back home. Write about a place you have visited after an absence of some time. Tell whether or not it changed and how you felt.

Similes and Metaphors

Steinbeck's writing is rich in **similes** and **metaphors**. A simile uses "like" or "as" to compare two things:

> "...plunged into the yellow sunlight like two swimmers hastening to get to shore."

A **metaphor** makes a more direct comparison:

> "The big tires sang a high note on the pavement."

Listed below are similes and metaphors from *The Grapes of Wrath*. For each one, write a new simile or metaphor comparing the subject to something different.

"...sow bugs like little armadillos,..." (p. 19)

"...on a neck as stringy and muscular as a celery stalk." (p. 24)

"...nails as thick and ridged as little clam shells." (p. 9)

"Snub-nosed monsters, raising the dust and sticking their snouts into it..." (p. 45)

"A large red drop of sun lingered on the horizon and then dripped over and was gone..." (p. 61)

"His bony hand dug its way like a squirrel into his overall pocket..." (p. 27)

Chapters 7 and 8

Level I

1. Skim the pages of the chapter to find some examples of the dishonest tactics used to sell cars to the tenant farmers.

2. What did the car salesman keep wishing he had? *(hundreds of jalopies)* Why? *(to sell to the departing, gullible farmers)*

3. What conclusion do Tom and Casy reach about Muley? *(that he's crazy)*

4. What happened to Uncle John that causes him so much guilt? *(He didn't go for the doctor when his wife was sick, and she died.)*

5. How does Uncle John try to make up for his "sin"? *(Gives things to people, especially to children.)*

6. How did Tom surprise his father? *(By sneaking up to the truck and just saying "Pa.")*

7. List phrases from page 95 that describe Ma. How important is she to the family? *(extremely important—its "citadel")*

8. Are Granma and Grampa fond of one another? *(yes)* How do you know? *(p. 100— "They... loved and needed the fighting.")*

9. How is Noah "different"? *(no emotions, seems misshapen)*

10. What secret does Pa have about Noah? *(He twisted and pulled him as he was being born because he was so nervous.)*

11. Was Casy's grace the usual sort? *(no)* Did it please Granma anyway? *(yes)*

12. Who is Rosasharn? *(Tom's sister, the oldest daughter of the Joads, actually named Rose of Sharon)* What is her situation? *(She is married to Connie Rivers and expecting a baby.)*

Level II

1. Have you ever gone to a store because of an advertised bargain that was gone when you got there? Did you buy something else that wasn't such a bargain?

2. Would you like to have the narrator of Chapter 7 as a friend? Why or why not?

3. Describe an adult you were "crazy about" as a young child. What made the person special?

4. If you hadn't seen your father in four years, how would you hope he would greet you? Was Tom's meeting with Pa like that?

5. How is your mother like Ma? How is she different?

6. Why did Ma almost lose control and then regain it when she saw Tommy? What would have happened if she had cried?

7. Compare Grampa and Granma to your own grandparents or to another elderly couple you know.

8. Who were the Hatfields and McCoys? How do they relate to this novel?

9. Why did Al admire Tom so much? How did it show?

Vocabulary

insubstantial (86)	prophecy (87)	supplication (104)	conjecture (104)
lithely (93)	incredulously (93)	intricacies (106)	rakishly (108)
animosity (94)	citadel (95)	imperturbability (96)	arbiter (96)
veneration (109)			

Writing/Speech Assignment

Study newspaper and television advertisements for used cars. Write your own "sales pitch" and present it to the class. To make the activity more interesting, have one of your classmates pose as a prospective buyer.

Chapters 9 and 10

Level I

1. What were the junk men buying in addition to the farmers' possessions? *(their junked lives)*

2. Does Ma have any doubts about California? *(yes)*

3. What advice does Tom give Ma? *(Take one day at a time.)*

4. Where will Casy go? *(with the Joads)*

5. Who are Ruthie and Winfield? *(the youngest Joads, 12 and 10, respectively)*

6. How much money did the Joads get for the goods they sold? *($18)* Why didn't they get more? *("Merchandising was a secret to them.")*

7. How much money do the Joads have, altogether? *($154)*

8. List the decisions made at the family conference. *(to take Casy, to take the dogs, to butcher the pigs)*

9. What treasures did Ma bring? *(ring, watch charm, earrings, one gold cuff link)*

10. What problem does Grampa present the family with the morning they are to leave? *(He says he isn't going.)* How do they solve it? *(drug him with earache medicine)*

Level II

1. What does "You're buying a sorrow that can't talk" mean?

2. If you were being pushed out of your home, what ten things would you want to take with you?

3. Do you think Tom gave Ma good advice?

4. What is Casy's purpose in going west?

5. What made Al feel so important and responsible? What have you been in charge of that makes you feel this way?

6. What does Ma's willingness to feed another mouth (Casy) tell you about her character?

7. Why do you think the Joads decided to start packing and to leave earlier than they had planned?

8. Ma's burning of the old letters and clippings is a symbol of what?

Vocabulary

inveterate (123)	voluptuous (123)	fatuously (127)
assailed (125)	stereopticon (128)	titular (130)
relinquished (131)	eminent (132)	restiveness (136)

Writing Assignment

At the end of Chapter 10, the Joads are on the road. What are some of the things that might happen to them? What do you think is most likely?

Chapters 11 and 12

Level I

1. What is the difference between a tractor and a horse? *(pp. 148-149)*

2. Who comes to the empty houses? *(little boys from town, cats, mice, weasels, bats, owls)*

3. Look at a road atlas and find Sallisaw, Oklahoma. Try to locate Highway 66. What seems to have replaced it as a major east-west road? *(I-40)*

4. Find the cities and towns listed on pages 151-152. Use the mileage scale or mileage chart to figure out how far it is from Sallisaw to the California border. *(approximately 1,200 miles)*

5. What kinds of car problems did the people going west have? *(bad tires, gaskets, leaky radiators, broken fan belts)*

6. What warnings do the people at service stations give the travelers? *(that people have come back from California and there aren't enough jobs)*

7. To what does Steinbeck compare the cars on Highway 66? *(wounded animals limping along)*

Level II

1. How is a man who merely cultivates someone else's land with a tractor different from one who lives on it and uses a plow and a horse?

2. Reread the last sentence on Chapter 11. What does this remind you of?

3. Why is Highway 66 called "the road of flight"?

4. What kinds of problems have you experienced with cars? In what ways do you think cars have improved since the 1930s?

5. Why was it so easy for service stations to take advantage of the people going west?

6. Why do the travelers keep going on the road to California in spite of the rumors of no work?

Vocabulary

tributary (151)   caravan (152)   apprehensively (152)

Writing Assignment

Do you think it's true that "a fella in business got to lie an' cheat"? Why or why not?

Name _____

In the box below each character's name, write a few descriptive phrases from the novel.

THE JOAD FAMILY

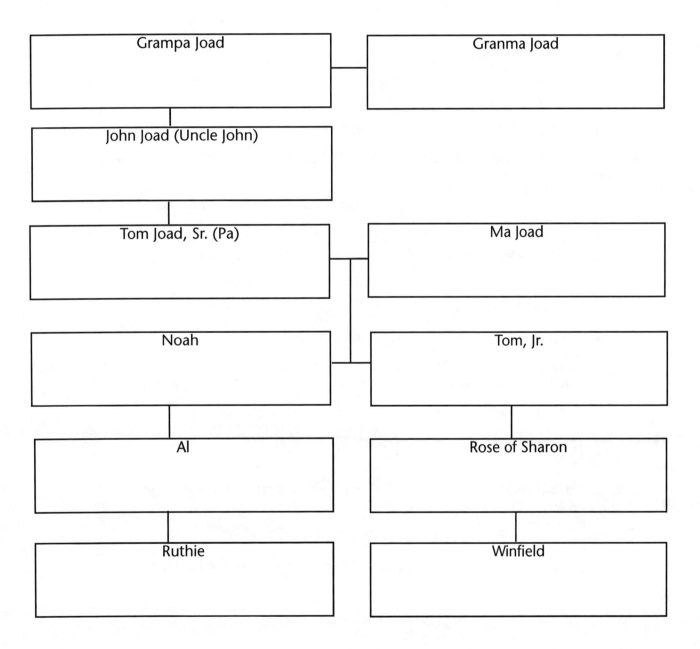

Grampa Joad	Granma Joad

John Joad (Uncle John)

Tom Joad, Sr. (Pa)	Ma Joad

Noah	Tom, Jr.

Al	Rose of Sharon

Ruthie	Winfield

Chapters 13 and 14

Level I

1. Did Ma tell Al she's afraid of going to California? *(no)* What is her main concern? *(meeting the family's needs)*

2. Why did Tom get angry at the fat man at the service station? *(The man thinks they are penniless bums and it hurts Tom's pride.)*

3. How do Rose of Sharon and Connie usually act when they are together? *(They live in their own secret world, and talk about all of their plans.)*

4. How did the Joads meet the Wilsons? *(camped next to them)* What happened that evening? *(Grampa died)*

5. Who does "black eyes that looked out of a well of horror" describe? *(Sairy Wilson)*

6. Why was it important to the Joads to help the Wilsons with their car? *(They had offered Grampa a sheltered place to die.)*

7. What do those who hate change fear the most? *(that people will join together and revolt)*

8. What makes the people in the Western states nervous? *(the migration of so many sharecroppers, especially since they are white, seventh-generation Americans)*

Level II

1. What did Steinbeck mean by "He had become the soul of the car"?

2. What things make Tom realize the fat man is really "one of them"?

3. With the exception of Rose of Sharon's concern for her baby, the family didn't have much reaction to the dog being run over. Why? How would you react if it was your dog?

4. Why do you think the government gets involved when people die?

5. Why did Casy say the Lord's Prayer as Grampa was dying? In Casy's opinion, Grampa was lucky. Why?

6. What did Casy mean when he said that Grampa was dying when he left the farm? Did he know he was sick?

7. What do you think is wrong with Sairy Wilson?

8. What one quality, according to Steinbeck, distinguishes Man from other animals?

Vocabulary

wizened (172)　　　timbre (172)　　　zygote (194)

Writing Assignment

Making men hate, fear, and suspect each other is often called the theory of "divide and conquer." It has often been used to control large groups of people. Think of an example from history or from your own experience and write about it.

Chapters 15 and 16

Level I

1. Why does Mae hate the rich people? *(they're snobs and leave poor tips)*

2. How does the behavior of the man with the two little boys compare to the way the Westerners think the migrants act? *(He's polite and humble; wants to buy just ten cents worth of the loaf and doesn't want charity. He's also kind-hearted, wanting the children to have a treat.)*

3. In what order did the Joads and Wilsons adjust to life on the road? *(from youngest to oldest)*

4. What is Rose of Sharon's main concern? *(that something will hurt the baby)* What do she and Connie plan? *(to live in town, and for Connie to study radio)*

5. Why doesn't Tom want to tell Al about jail? *(When he was there, he was never sure if he was crazy or not.)*

6. Describe the man at the junkyard. *(He had only one eye, and the socket of the other was exposed. He was covered with grease and felt very sorry for himself.)*

7. What is Al worried about? *(that everyone will think he caused the car trouble by driving it "wrong")*

Level II

1. Both Chapter 15 and Chapter 2 are about hamburger joints on the road. How are they different in point-of-view?

2. How are Mae, Al, and the truck drivers all sympathetic toward those who have less than they do?

3. Give an example of Al's accepted "ritualized thievery."

4. Do you think it would really cost Connie nothing to send off for a course?

5. Why does Ma react so violently to Tom's idea of the others going ahead while the car is being fixed?

6. What did Pa lose by giving in to Ma?

7. When Al and Tom went to town for the car part, how did Tom behave more responsibly than Al?

8. Do you think Tom's remarks to the junk yard man were unkind?

9. Why do you think Al tried to hit the cat on the road? Would Tom have done it? How do you know?

Vocabulary

vivaciousness (197)	morosely (201)	querulously (247)
quoit (198)	relapsed (227)	derelicts (228)
languid (198)	lanky (239)	accouterments (198)
vagrants (240)		

Speech Assignment

Check your family's mail, the newspaper, and television ads. Find an example of misleading advertising that sounds as if you will get something for free. Prepare a brief oral report explaining what the company is really trying to get from the consumer.

Chapters 17 and 18

Level I

1. Why did the people going West huddle together at night? *(They were comforted by having so much in common.)*

2. What "code" developed in the camps. *(See page 250.)* What were the punishments for breaking it? *(a fight or ostracism)*

3. What did the men talk about? *(their land, their tragedies, their futures)*

4. On a map, find the New Mexico-Arizona border and locate the Painted Desert.

5. What was good about the arrival in California? *(the cool river)* What was bad? *(Granma was getting worse; the police told them to leave and treated Ma badly.)*

6. What does "Okie" mean? *(It orignially meant someone from Oklahoma, but the Westerners used it in a derogatory way to describe all of the migrants.)*

7. What did Noah do in Needles, California? *(He decided to stay by the river and simply walked away.)*

8. How did Sairy Wilson describe herself? *("pain covered with skin")*

Level II

1. Discuss: "...the songs, which were all of the people, were sung in the nights."

2. Why did the people need to "build worlds" at night?

3. What does Casy say about people who "collect things like prairie dogs"?

4. Why didn't Ma want the Jehovites to come and pray over Granma? How did she feel later?

5. What do you think Steinbeck meant when he wrote that Ma was "fighting with her face"?

6. Why does having dirty clothes and not even washing the potatoes seem so terrible to Ma?

7. Casy says he has no God. Do you think he does?

8. What very strong thing did Ma do during the trip across the desert?

Vocabulary

ostracism (251)	exhortation (272)	vehemence (261)
feral (272)	tule (261)	decorous (278)
prosperous (262)	flailing (287)	

Writing

Tom said, "It don't take no nerve to do somepin when there ain't nothin' else you can do." Write a paragraph explaining what he meant. Give an example from personal experience if you can.

Chapters 19 and 20

Level I

1. How did Americans come to own land in California? *(by stealing it from the Mexicans)*

2. What hunger did the new owners' children lack? *(the hunger to own land)*

3. How did farming become industry? *(It became big and impersonal.)*

4. What bothered Ma most about Granma's death? *(She had to be buried by the county with no funeral.)*

5. Describe the Hooverville. *(pp. 310-311)*

6. What is a blacklist? *(People who talk about organizing are blacklisted and prevented from working.)*

7. How did Rose of Sharon scare Connie? *(by demanding a house)*

8. What sad event involved the camp's children? *(Ma didn't have enough stew to share.)*

9. What did Floyd ask of the labor contractor? *(a written work order with wages stated)* Were his demands fair?

When the migrant families were still on their farms, they had certain needs and fears. When they were on the road, their needs and fears changed. Complete the chart below for each situation.

On the Farm	On The Road
Needs:	Needs:
Fears:	Fears:

Level II

1. Why did the Okies find so much hatred when they came to California?

2. Discuss: "Repression works only to strengthen and knit the repressed."

3. Floyd fills Tom in on the methods used by the labor contractors to get men to work cheaply. Explain.

4. How do you think Tom's attitude toward police developed? How might it get him into trouble?

5. Why does Casy welcome the chance to take the blame for Tom?

6. Why did Uncle John find it necessary to go get drunk?

7. Do you think the Joads should have gone to Tulare?

8. What do you think happened to Connie?

Vocabulary

horde (297)	dispossessed (299)	intimidate (307)
slovenly (311)	speculatively (313)	disconsolate (336)
servile (359)		

Writing

Ma Joad tells Tom, "We're the people—we go on." (p. 360) Reread the rest of her speech on this subject. Do you agree that the rich die out but the poor go on? Support your opinion.

Chapters 21 and 22

Level I

1. How were the small farmers in California eventually hurt by the big companies? *(They too were pushed off their land due to the business tactics of cannery owners.)*

2. There is a thin line between hunger and _____. *(anger)*

3. What is Ma most anxious to do at the government camp? *(laundry)*

4. How do the camp residents pay to stay at the government camp if they have no money? *(They work around the camp.)*

5. What was Hines' definition of a "red"? *(someone who wants 30 cents an hour when they're paying 25 cents)*

6. What embarrassing thing happened to Ma? *(She went into the men's side of the sanitary unit.)*

7. What is the camp manager like? *(friendly and sympathetic)*

8. How does the "deep down Jesus lover" scare Rose of Sharon? *(She tells her that dancing is a sin and will cause the baby to be damaged or born dead.)*

Level II

1. What does Steinbeck mean by "the ridiculousness of the industrial life"?

2. Why were the migrants willing to work for so little? What do you think would have happened if they all refused?

3. How were the people in the government camp different from those at the Hoovervilles? How were they the same?

4. What made Mr. Thomas reduce the pay to 25 cents an hour? Did he have a choice?

5. What effect has the Joad adventure had on Ruthie and Winfield? What needs do they have that aren't being met?

6. How are Jim Rawley and Casy alike?

7. Why did the frayed seams of Jim Rawley's coat reassure Ma?

8. Now that the Joads have a decent place to live, Ma is sometimes sad. Why?

Vocabulary

agrarian (362)	ravenous (364)	destitute (368)
contrite (385)	delusion (397)	reverential (403)

Writing Assignment

Mrs. Joyce was ashamed to get groceries on credit because she felt it would be taking charity. Write your own defintion of charity. Describe someone you think is a charitable person.

Chapters 23 and 24

Level I

1. The migrant people had another kind of hunger. What was it? *(a hunger for amusement)* How did they satisfy it? *(story telling, a movie instead of food, getting drunk, music, dancing)*

2. Who is Ezra Houston? *(chairman of the Central Committee)*

3. What do the local people plan to do to get rid of the migrants? *(get a fight started at the dance so the sheriff can intervene and claim the disorderly camp should be shut down)*

4. What did the Jesus-lovers do during the dance? *(they watched in contempt)*

5. What is school like for the few migrant children who attend? *(Other kids call them names and fight with them.)*

6. How did the troublemakers justify their actions? *(They said they needed the money to feed their families.)*

Level II

1. Reread paragraphs 5 and 6 on page 423 aloud. Listen to the rhythm of the words. What is this literary technique called? *(onomatopoeia)*

2. Why did Steinbeck include the paragraphs about the preacher on pages 424-425?

3. In what ways do the Okies contribute to the economy? In what ways do *you* contribute to today's economy?

4. Why do you think Rose of Sharon was so reluctant to go to the dance?

5. In what ways is Al like some 16-year-old boys you know?

6. What does "on the faces of the watchers the smiles were of old times" mean?

7. Why did the "turkey shoot" in Akron stop the protest over the union?

Vocabulary

radical (420)   contemptuous (431)   pinioned (441)

Writing

Steinbeck describes the dance in detail in Chapter 24. Write several paragraphs describing a dance you have attended. Try to imitate Steinbeck's writing style.

Activity

Discuss with the students the differences between necessities and luxuries, and how different people perceive them. You might compare a primitive tribe's necessities with those of a wealthy family. Then have the students make their own "Needs and Wants" charts like the one below. Have them consider categories like housing, a place to sleep, food, entertainment, clothing, and education.

My Family	The Joad Family
Necessities:	Necessities:
Luxuries:	Luxuries:

Using Character Webs in the Novel Unit Approach

Attribute Webs are simply a visual representation of a character from the novel. They provide a systematic way for the students to organize and recap the information they have about a particular character. Attribute webs may be used after reading the novel to recapitulate information about a particular character or completed gradually as information unfolds, done individually, or finished as a group project.

One type of character attribute web uses these divisions:
- How a character acts and feels. (How does the character feel in this picture? How would you feel if this happened to you? How do you think the character feels?)
- How a character looks. (Close your eyes and picture the character. Describe him to me.)
- Where a character lives. (Where and when does the character live?)
- How others feel about the character. (How does another specific character feel about our character?)

In group discussion about the student attribute webs and specific characters, the teacher can ask for backup proof from the novel. You can also include inferential thinking.
Attribute webs need not be confined to characters. They may also be used to organize information about a concept, object or place.

Attribute Web

The attribute web below is designed to help you gather clues the author provides about what a character is like. Fill in the blanks with words and phrases which tell how the character acts and looks, as well as what the character says and what others say about him or her.

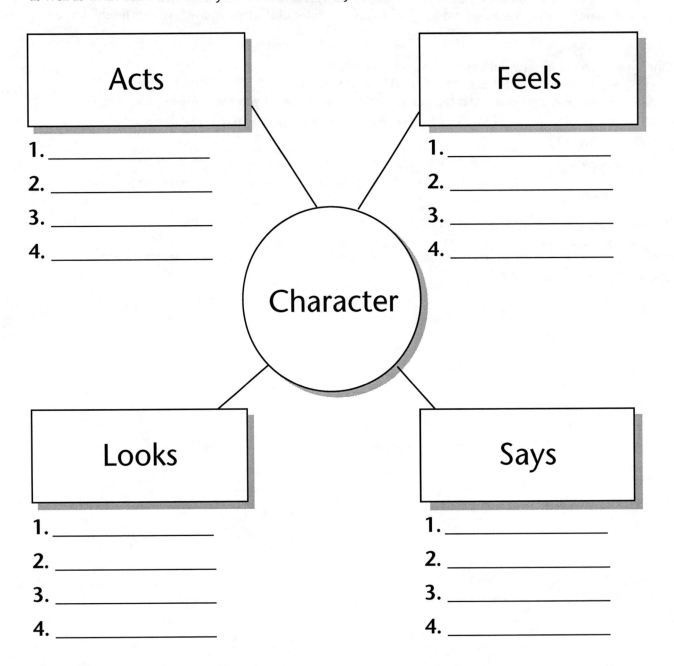

Acts

1. _____
2. _____
3. _____
4. _____

Feels

1. _____
2. _____
3. _____
4. _____

Character

Looks

1. _____
2. _____
3. _____
4. _____

Says

1. _____
2. _____
3. _____
4. _____

Attribute Web

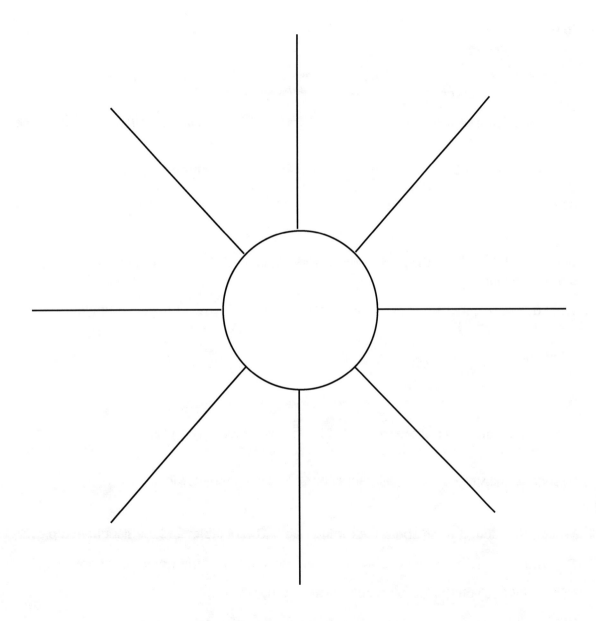

Chapters 25 and 26

Level I

1. To what does Steinbeck compare the California valleys in the spring? *("fragrant pink and white waters in a shallow sea")*

2. Why did the fruit described in Chapter 25 have to rot? *(The small farmers couldn't pay wages to pick it when the big canneries were offering such low prices for it.)*

3. Why did they make such bad wine from the grapes? *(They couldn't afford to make good wine because people couldn't afford to buy it.)*

4. What did Ma insist the men do after a few weeks at the government camp? *(figure out what to do next; talk it out)* How did Pa react? *(He was angry and embarrassed that Ma had taken over his power.)*

5. Why did Ma want to make Pa angry? *(to get him to act)*

6. What scares Tom about the Hoovervilles? *(He's afraid he'll get mad and kill someone if they live in a place like that.)*

7. What did Willie, Jule, and Tom talk about just before the Joads left the government camp? *(organizing a union)*

8. What announcement did Al make on the way to Bakersfield? *(He's planning to go out on his own soon.)*

9. What made Ma so angry at the company's store? *(the high prices)*

10. Who was the organizer of the strike outside Hooper's Ranch? *(Casy)* What happened to him? *(He was killed by one of the anti-union vigilantes.)* What did Tom do? *(killed one of the vigilantes)*

11. As soon as the strike broke, what happened? *(The wages were cut in half.)*

Level II

1. What is the saddest thing about the rotting fruit and vegetables and the slaughtered pigs?

2. Discuss the last sentence on Chapter 25. What do you think "the vintage" symbolizes?

3. Which child do you think is Ma Joad's favorite? Why?

4. Why did Ma choose this particular time to pierce Rose of Sharon's ears?

5. Will Al really be coming back to the blonde girl at the government camp?

6. Would the Joads still have gone through the gate at the Hooper Ranch if they'd fully understood what was going on outside?

7. What can you tell about the storekeeper's character from his actions: loaning Ma a dime for the sugar, cuddling his cat. Is he "one of the people" or one of the enemy?

8. Why do the guards at the gate hope the strike goes on? Whose side should they really be on?

9. Just before he died, Casy said "You fellas don't know what you're doin'." Later on, Ma says she wishes Granma could have heard him say it. Explain what Ma meant and who Casy symbolizes.

10. Ma says she's getting mean. Name some other ways the grapes of hope are changing to grapes of wrath for the Joads.

Vocabulary

preventive (446)	forlornly (475)	vigilantes (493)
denunciation (449)	docilely (476)	confidentially (472)
pall (475)	menacingly (481)	obscure (486)

Writing Assignment

Ma usually keeps up the rest of the family's spirits and assures them that everything will be all right. On page 503, she explains how she really feels. How does her explanation make her previous behavior seem even more heroic?

Chapters 27 and 28

Level I

1. Why do the cotton pickers always argue with the scale man? *(They think his scales are fixed. He thinks they put rocks in their cotton bags.)*

2. Why is it important for the people to save some of the money from cotton picking? *(Winter is coming, and there will be no work.)*

3. What is nice about the Joads' boxcar home? *(leakproof and not drafty)*

4. What "luxuries" do the wages from cotton picking provide? *(meat on the table every night, a tin stove, new overalls, a dress for Ma, milk, sirup, new frying pan)*

5. Is it necessary for Ma and Pa to talk to Al about Aggie? Explain. *(No. Al announces that he and Aggie plan to get married anyway.)*

6. The 20-acre cotton picking site was picked out by noon. Why? *(There were too many pickers desperate to make a little money.)*

7. What was the result of Rose of Sharon's insistence on going with the family to pick cotton? *(She caught a chill.)*

Level II

1. What made cotton picking good work?

2. The Joads are "aristocrats" in the boxcar camp. Where do the aristocrats in your community live?

3. Why didn't Ma get angry at Ruthie for telling the other children about Tom?

4. Reread page 537. What are Tom's dreams now? What is Ma's hope for Tom?

5. How does Ma explain her ability to cope with change better than Pa does? (pp. 541-542)

6. Why did Rose of Sharon crawl into the bushes after hearing Al's news?

Vocabulary

placards (520)	inquisitive (521)	aristocrats (525)
cynically (531)	majestically (531)	effluvium (532)
patina (539)		

Writing Assignment

Al and Aggie are 16. Does this seem "grown up" to you as it does to their parents? Do you think 16 is old enough to get married?

Chapters 29 and 30

Level I

1. What is the "greatest terror" of all? *(no work for three months)*

2. What came with the rain, cold, and lack of work? *(disease, starvation, death)*

3. What happened where a number of men gathered together? *(Fear changed to anger.)*

4. Why did the Joads have to stay at the boxcar camp even though the water in the creek was rising? *(Rose of Sharon went into labor.)*

5. What happened to the truck? *(It got too wet and the motor wouldn't start.)*

6. What happened to the embankment the men built? *(It collapsed.)*

7. What happened to Rose of Sharon's baby? *(It was born dead.)*

8. How are the events in questions 5, 6, and 7 above symbolic of what is happening in society as a whole at this time? *(machinery is the enemy; hopes and dreams collapse; children are dying)*

Level II

1. Why did the people in the "tight houses" hate the migrants? Why didn't the migrant people go on relief?

2. What would keep the men from breaking?

3. Putting something sharp under the mattress to cut birth pains is an old wives' tale. Can you think of some others?

4. How do you think the dead truck motor made Al feel? How did he show his growing sense of responsibility by taking charge of another situation?

5. What did Uncle John mean when he placed the dead baby in the water and said, "That's the way you can talk." What effect do you imagine the baby had on those who eventually found it?

6. How did Ruthie's anger show itself?

7. How does Rose of Sharon's act of kindness in the final scene of the novel show that the people will go on? How does it correlate with Ma's statement, "Use' ta be the fambly was fust. It ain't so now. Now it's anybody."

8. What do you think Steinbeck's novel says about the family of man? Do you think his philosophy applies to today's world? Who are the "oppressed" today? How can they be helped?

Vocabulary

tempo (553)   cringe (555)   engulfed (554)
levee (563)

Writing Assignment

When the novel ends, the Joads' situation seems totally hopeless. They have no food, no money, no work, and no transportation. What is the worst that could happen to them? What is the best that could happen?

Changes

The Joads' experiences changed all of the major characters in some way. Next to each character listed, tell how he or she changed and explain the causes of the changes.

Pa Joad:

Ma Joad:

Tom:

Al:

Rose of Sharon:

Jim Casy:

Project Ideas

1. Skim the pages of *The Grapes of Wrath* to make a list of things the Joads bought and how much they paid for them. Then consult a newspaper and find today's prices for similar items. Make an illustrated poster showing the price comparisons.

2. Analyze the nutritional value of the Joads' daily diet by listing a typical day's menu (when they had money for food) and finding the grams of protein, carbohydrates, and fat for each food. Also categorize each food by group: fruit, vegetable, grain, meat, dairy. What is wrong with the Joads' diet? Which food groups are missing or poorly represented? What is the fat content?

3. Read a biography of Cesar Chavez, the founder of the National Farm Workers' Association. Draw parallels between Chavez' family and the Joads. Write a summary of your conclusions.

4. Rose of Sharon received no prenatal care. Find out what she should have done if the family could have afforded it, and why prenatal care is so important. Make a poster showing what expectant mothers should and should not do.

5. The illustration on the front cover of the novel is by William Low. Use charcoal, watercolors, or pastels to design your own cover illustration for *The Grapes of Wrath*.

6. With a partner or group, choose an important scene from *The Grapes of Wrath* and write a script for dramatization. Present the skit to your class. Include an explanation of why you think the scene is important to the novel.

7. Listen to the lyrics of some songs from the '30s, or consult songbooks in your library to read the lyrics. Find several songs that reflect how people felt about economic conditions. Play the songs for your classmates, or read the words aloud.

8. Find pictures of 1930s cars like the ones the migrant people drove to California. Learn how these old cars worked differently than the ones we have today. Give an oral report on your findings.

9. Find out how modern farming techniques prevent dust storms, crop flooding, and soil exhaustion. Look for information on crop rotation and terracing. Write a report on your findings.

Essay Topics

1. How is *The Grapes of Wrath* a novel about the struggle between good and evil?

2. Compare the living conditions and lifestyles of Steinbeck's migrant families with those of today's migrant workers.

3. Explain how the behavior of the Joads shows Steinbeck's view of the responsibility of the individual to society as a whole.

4. Show how Ma Joad proves her strength again and again.

5. In what ways is Pa Joad a victim of circumstances he cannot control or understand? Compare and contrast his life as a migrant with his life as a farmer.

6. Trace Tom Joad's spiritual progress throughout the novel.

7. How does Steinbeck portray Casy as a Christ-like figure?

8. How do the various members of the Joad family influence one another and cause action to be taken by the family because of one member?

9. How do the various settings in The Grapes of Wrath contribute to the theme?

10. Choose any character in *The Grapes of Wrath* and trace his/her internal conflict throughout the novel.

11. Analyze three of Steinbeck's most effective extended metaphors in terms of their contribution to the theme of the novel.

12. What is the central idea or theme of *The Grapes of Wrath*? Support your opinion with facts, details, and examples.

13. Read one of Steinbeck's shorter novels (*Of Mice and Men* or *Cannery Row*) and compare its characters with those in *The Grapes of Wrath*.

14. Steinbeck tells the story of the migrants from many different points of view. Compare and contrast these points of view.

15. The intercalary chapters are about what is happening to the migrants in general. Analyze these chapters in terms of Steinbeck's purpose.

Bibliography

The following books may be helpful to you and your students in your study of *The Grapes of Wrath*.

Coles, Robert. Migrants, *Sharecroppers, Mountaineers.* Boston: Little, Brown & Co., 1971.

Gregory, James Noble. *American Exodus: the Dust Bowl Migration and Okie Culture in California.* New York: Oxford University Press, 1989. (Especially useful for its black-and-white photos of actual Okies.)

Hobhouse, Henry. *Seeds of Change: Five Plants that Transformed Mankind.* New York: Harper and Row, 1986.

Heinrichs, Ann. *Oklahoma.* Chicago: Children's Press, 1989.

Essay Evaluation Form

1. **Focus:** Student writes a clear thesis and includes it in the opening paragraph.

10	8	4

2. **Organization:** The final draft reflects the assigned outline; transitions are used to link ideas.

20	16	12

3. **Support:** Adequate details are provided; extraneous details are omitted.

12	10	7

4. **Detail:** Each quote or reference is explained (as if the teacher had not read the book); ideas are not redundant.

12	10	7

5. **Mechanics:** Spelling, capitalization, and usage are correct.

16	12	8

6. **Sentence Structure:** The student avoids run-ons and sentence fragments.

10	8	4

7. **Verb:** All verbs are in the correct tense; sections in which plot is summarized are in the present tense.

10	8	4

8. **Total effect of the essay.**

10	8	4

100	80	50

Comments:

Total: _____

(This rubric may be altered to fit the needs of a particular class. You may wish to show it to students before they write their essays. They can use it as a self-evaluation tool, and they will be aware of exactly how their essays will be graded.)

Notes

Notes